Expressive Reflections
Exploring Emotions Through Art, Writing, and Meditation

This book is Dedicated to:

_____

Reflections in Water

Exploring emotions through watercolor painting or mixed media techniques

Create a serene environment in your art space. Reflect on your emotions and select a color palette that represents those feelings. Experiment with watercolor techniques to create abstract or representational artworks that reflect your emotional state. Embrace the fluidity of watercolors and let your emotions guide your brushstrokes. Take time to observe and reflect on the emotions that arise during the painting process.

Sketches and Ideas

Reflections in Water

Find a quiet and peaceful space. Close your eyes and imagine yourself surrounded by serene water. Focus on the gentle movement and reflections. Take deep breaths and let the calmness wash over you.

Reflect on the emotions that arise as you envision reflections in water. Consider how the fluidity and transparency of water can mirror your own emotions and provide a metaphorical canvas for expression.

Rhythm and Movement

Using dance and rhythmic patterns to express and release emotions

Find a spacious and uninterrupted area to move freely. Explore different rhythmic patterns and movements that resonate with your emotions. Allow the music or silence to guide your body as you express and release your emotions through dance. Engage in improvisation and let your body naturally respond to the emotions within you. Reflect on the sensations, energy, and emotions experienced during the dance session.

Sketches and Ideas

Rhythm and Movement

Find a comfortable place to sit or stand. Close your eyes and tune in to your breath. Start moving your body in a slow, rhythmic manner, syncing your movements to your breath. Allow the rhythm to guide you and explore different movements.

Reflect on the sensations and emotions that emerged as you engaged in rhythmic movement. Consider how movement can serve as a gateway to expressing and releasing emotions, and how it connects your body and mind.

Storytelling through Collage

Creating collages that tell a narrative or reflect personal experiences

Collect a variety of images, photos, and other materials that evoke different emotions or represent aspects of your personal experiences. Arrange and layer these materials to create collages that tell a story or visually depict significant moments in your life. Use your creativity to explore symbolism and composition in conveying emotions and narratives through collage. Reflect on the stories and emotions captured in your collages and how they resonate with your own experiences.

Sketches and Ideas

Storytelling through Collage

Settle in a quiet space. Take a few deep breaths to ground yourself. Gather old magazines, scissors, and glue. As you browse through the magazines, let your intuition guide you to images that resonate with you. Cut them out and arrange them on a piece of paper, creating a collage that tells a story.

Reflect on the story that emerged through your collage. Consider the emotions and memories evoked by the images and how they interconnect. Reflect on the narrative you have created and the significance it holds for you.

The Art of Sound

Using soundscapes or music composition to evoke and process emotions

Find a quiet and comfortable space to immerse yourself in sound. Create soundscapes by combining different sounds, such as nature sounds, instrumental music, or ambient noises, to evoke specific emotions. Alternatively, compose your own music that reflects your current emotional state. Close your eyes, listen attentively, and allow the sounds to stir emotions within you. Reflect on the emotions evoked by the soundscape or composition and explore how sound can be a powerful medium for emotional expression and processing.

Sketches and Ideas

The Art of Sound

Find a comfortable position and close your eyes. Focus on your breath, allowing yourself to settle into the present moment. Start playing calming music or nature sounds. As you listen, pay attention to the sensations, emotions, and imagery that arise within you.

Reflect on the emotional journey you experienced while listening to the sounds. Consider how sound can evoke specific emotions and transport you to different mental and emotional landscapes. Reflect on any insights or inspirations that emerged from this sensory experience.

Expressive Body Art

Exploring body painting or temporary tattoos as a form of self-expression

Set aside a dedicated space where you can comfortably engage in body art. Use body-safe paints or temporary tattoo materials to create designs or patterns on your body that reflect your emotions or personal symbolism. Embrace your body as a canvas for self-expression and allow the process of painting or adorning your body to be a mindful and intentional act of embracing and expressing your emotions. Take time to observe and reflect on the emotions and messages conveyed through your body art.

Sketches and Ideas

Expressive Body Art

Find a quiet space where you can move freely. Stand or sit comfortably and close your eyes. Connect with your breath and your body. Begin to move, allowing your body to express itself in whatever way feels natural. Let go of self-judgment and let your body guide you.

Reflect on the emotions, sensations, and messages that your body expressed through movement. Consider how the process of expressive body art helped you tap into a deeper level of self-awareness and emotional release.

Emotional Landscapes

Painting or drawing landscapes that reflect inner emotional states

Find inspiration from landscapes in nature, photographs, or your imagination. Use painting or drawing techniques to create landscapes that visually represent your inner emotional states. Explore the colors, brushstrokes, and composition that resonate with your emotions. Allow the process of creating emotional landscapes to be a meditative and reflective experience. Observe and reflect on the emotions and sensations that arise during the artistic process and contemplate the connections between your inner world and the external world portrayed in your artwork.

Sketches and Ideas

Emotional Landscapes

Find a quiet and peaceful space where you won't be interrupted. Close your eyes and take a few deep breaths to center yourself. Imagine a vast landscape in your mind, reflecting the emotions you want to explore. Observe the details and let the emotions flow through this landscape.

Reflect on the emotional landscape you envisioned. Consider the colors, textures, and elements that emerged in your mind. Reflect on the emotions that were present and the insights gained from exploring these inner landscapes.

Abstract Poetry

Experimenting with abstract language and metaphor to express emotions in poetic form

Set aside time to write poetry in a quiet and introspective space. Experiment with abstract language, metaphors, and symbolism to convey your emotions in poetic form. Allow your creativity to flow freely and explore new ways of expressing your feelings through words. Reflect on the emotions conveyed in your poetry and how the abstract language and metaphors capture the depth and nuances of your inner world. Consider how poetry can serve as a powerful tool for emotional expression and self-reflection.

Sketches and Ideas

Abstract Poetry

Find a quiet and comfortable place to sit. Close your eyes and take a few deep breaths to calm your mind. Let your thoughts and emotions flow freely. When you feel ready, open your eyes and write a poem without focusing on structure or rhyme. Let the words and emotions guide your pen.

Reflect on the emotions and thoughts that emerged through your abstract poetry. Consider the freedom of expression and the unique language you used to convey your emotions. Reflect on the meaning and significance behind the words and phrases you chose.

Ceramic Therapy

Using clay and pottery techniques to explore and express emotions

Set up a pottery studio or workspace with the necessary tools and materials. Use clay to create ceramic pieces that reflect your emotions, whether through sculpting, molding, or wheel throwing techniques. Allow the tactile nature of clay to be a therapeutic experience as you shape and form your emotions into tangible artworks. Reflect on the process of working with clay, the sensations experienced, and the emotions expressed through your ceramic creations. Consider how the medium of clay can facilitate emotional exploration and provide a sense of release and healing.

Sketches and Ideas

Ceramic Therapy

Find a quiet and comfortable space where you can work with clay. Take a moment to ground yourself by taking a few deep breaths. As you work with the clay, pay attention to the sensations, textures, and shapes that you create. Let your hands guide you.

Reflect on the experience of working with clay and the emotions that surfaced during the process. Consider the connection between your hands and the clay as a means of expressing and shaping emotions. Reflect on the transformative nature of clay therapy and its impact on your well-being.

Art Therapy Mandalas

Creating mandalas specifically for therapeutic purposes and emotional exploration

Set aside a calm and focused space for creating mandalas. Use various art materials, such as colored pencils, markers, or paints, to design and fill in mandala patterns. Allow the process of creating mandalas to be meditative and mindful. Explore different colors, shapes, and patterns that resonate with your emotions and inner state. Reflect on the therapeutic benefits of creating mandalas, the symbolism embedded in your designs, and the emotions and insights that arise during the mandala-making process.

Sketches and Ideas

Art Therapy Mandalas

Find a quiet and calm space where you can work on creating a mandala. Take a few deep breaths to center yourself. As you create the mandala, let your intuition guide your color and pattern choices. Focus on the meditative process of creating and the symbolic meaning of the mandala.

Reflect on the emotions and thoughts that arose during the creation of your mandala. Consider the symbolism and personal meaning behind the colors, patterns, and shapes you used. Reflect on the meditative and therapeutic aspects of working with mandalas.

Movement and Stillness

Using photography to capture the juxtaposition of movement and stillness in daily life

Find moments of movement and stillness in your daily life. Use a camera or smartphone to capture photographs that represent these contrasting states. Experiment with different compositions, lighting, and perspectives to convey the emotions associated with movement and stillness. Reflect on the captured photographs and the emotions evoked by the juxtaposition of movement and stillness. Consider how photography can serve as a powerful medium for expressing and exploring emotions through visual storytelling.

Sketches and Ideas

Movement and Stillness

Find a peaceful and open space where you can observe your surroundings. Take a few deep breaths to ground yourself. Observe the movement and stillness around you. Pay attention to the contrast and the emotions they evoke within you.

Reflect on the interplay between movement and stillness that you observed. Consider how these contrasting elements reflect your own emotional states and the balance between activity and tranquility in your life.

Found Poetry

Creating poems or stories by rearranging words and phrases from existing texts

Select a book, magazine, or newspaper as a source for found poetry. Read through the chosen text and select words or phrases that resonate with your emotions. Rearrange and combine these words and phrases to create poems or stories that capture the essence of your emotions or convey specific narratives. Reflect on the found poetry you have created and the emotions it evokes. Consider how found poetry allows you to reinterpret existing texts and find new meaning and expression through the rearrangement of words.

Sketches and Ideas

Found Poetry

Find a comfortable place to sit with a book or a piece of writing. Take a few deep breaths to center yourself. Read through the text and allow certain words or phrases to catch your attention. Rearrange these words and phrases to create a new poem or story.

Reflect on the process of creating found poetry. Consider the emotions and meanings that emerged from the rearranged words and phrases. Reflect on how this unique form of expression allowed you to uncover new insights and connections within the original text.

Textured Emotions

Exploring texture and tactile materials to represent different emotions visually

Gather a variety of textured materials such as fabric, paper, yarn, or natural elements. Use these materials to create textured artworks that visually represent different emotions. Experiment with layering, collage techniques, or mixed media approaches to convey the sensory experience of emotions. Reflect on the textures and materials used in your artwork and how they evoke or symbolize different emotions. Consider how texture can deepen the emotional impact and add a tactile dimension to your artistic expressions.

Sketches and Ideas

Textured Emotions

Find a quiet space where you can explore different tactile materials. Take a few deep breaths to center yourself. Choose a variety of textured materials, such as fabrics, papers, or natural elements. Allow yourself to freely touch and arrange these materials to represent your emotions.

Reflect on the textures and materials you used to represent your emotions. Consider how the tactile experience of working with different textures enhanced your emotional expression. Reflect on the unique qualities of texture as a medium for conveying emotions.

Soulful Portraits

Creating expressive portraits that capture the essence of a person's emotions and inner world

Choose a subject for your portrait, whether it's yourself, a loved one, or a fictional character. Use various artistic techniques, such as drawing, painting, or mixed media, to create a portrait that goes beyond physical likeness and captures the essence of the subject's emotions and inner world. Reflect on the emotions and personality traits you aim to convey in the portrait. Consider how portraiture can serve as a powerful means of capturing and expressing the depth of human emotions.

Sketches and Ideas

Soulful Portraits

Find a quiet and comfortable space to sit and reflect. Close your eyes and take a few deep breaths to center yourself. Visualize a person or a character who represents an emotion or inner state you want to explore. Open your eyes and begin drawing their portrait.

Reflect on the emotions and characteristics that emerged while drawing the soulful portrait. Consider the connection between the visual representation and the essence of the emotion or inner state you aimed to capture. Reflect on any insights gained from this artistic exploration.

Nature's Healing Touch

Using natural materials such as leaves, flowers, or stones in art to symbolize healing and growth

Engage in nature walks or spend time outdoors to collect natural materials like leaves, flowers, or stones. Use these materials in your artworks to symbolize healing, growth, or connection with the natural world. Reflect on the symbolism of the natural materials and how they evoke emotions of healing, vitality, or tranquility. Consider how the integration of nature into art can deepen the emotional resonance and provide a sense of grounding and harmony.

Sketches and Ideas

Nature's Healing Touch

Find a tranquil outdoor setting in nature, such as a garden, park, or forest. Take a moment to connect with your breath and the natural surroundings. As you explore, collect leaves, flowers, or stones that resonate with you. Arrange them into a meaningful composition.

Reflect on the process of gathering and arranging natural materials. Consider the symbolic meaning and healing properties associated with the elements you chose. Reflect on the calming and rejuvenating effects of nature and the role it played in your creative process.

Collage Journaling

Combining collage techniques with journaling prompts to explore emotions and memories

Set up a dedicated journaling space and gather various materials like magazines, photographs, paper, and art supplies. Use collage techniques to create visual representations of your emotions and memories in your journal. Combine the collages with reflective journaling prompts to explore and process your emotions and experiences. Reflect on the collages and journal entries, considering the connections between visual expression and written reflection. How does the combination of collage and journaling enhance your exploration of emotions and memories?

Sketches and Ideas

Collage Journaling

Find a quiet and comfortable space where you can focus. Take a few deep breaths to center yourself. Gather old magazines, scissors, glue, and a journal. As you browse through the magazines, cut out images and words that resonate with your emotions or memories. Arrange them in your journal along with your own reflections and writings.

Reflect on the collage journaling process. Consider the emotions, memories, and themes that emerged through the selection and arrangement of images and words. Reflect on the insights gained and the connections made during the journaling process.

Sacred Geometry

Creating artwork inspired by geometric patterns to explore the harmony of emotions and thoughts

Research and explore different geometric patterns and their symbolic meanings. Use these patterns as inspiration for creating artwork that reflects the harmony of emotions and thoughts. Experiment with various art mediums, such as drawing, painting, or digital art, to bring these geometric patterns to life. Reflect on the emotions and thoughts evoked by working with sacred geometry and how the balance and symmetry of the patterns resonate with your inner state. Consider how sacred geometry can be a tool for self-reflection and achieving inner harmony through artistic expression.

Sketches and Ideas

Sacred Geometry

Find a quiet and peaceful space where you can focus. Close your eyes and take a few deep breaths to center yourself. Visualize geometric patterns such as circles, triangles, or spirals. Imagine these patterns expanding and connecting in intricate ways.

Reflect on the sacred geometry visualization. Consider the emotions, thoughts, and sensations that arose during the visualization. Reflect on the symbolic meaning and significance of the geometric patterns and their impact on your emotional and mental state.

Shadow Play

Using light and shadow to visually express different emotions and their complexities

Set up a space with a light source and objects to cast shadows. Manipulate the lighting to create different shadow shapes and forms. Experiment with arranging objects and capturing the interplay of light and shadow to visually express various emotions and their complexities. Reflect on the emotions evoked by the interplay of light and shadow. Consider how shadows can convey a sense of depth, mystery, or hidden emotions in visual art.

Sketches and Ideas

Shadow Play

Find a dimly lit space where you can observe the interplay of light and shadow. Take a few deep breaths to center yourself. Observe how the light casts shadows and shapes in the environment. Pay attention to the emotions and associations that arise as you observe the shifting patterns.

Reflect on the experience of observing light and shadow play. Consider the emotions, symbolism, or metaphors that emerged from the interplay of light and shadow. Reflect on the transitory nature of shadows and the insights gained through this visual exploration.

Artistic Alchemy

Experimenting with different art mediums and techniques to transform emotions into creative energy

Explore a range of art mediums and techniques, such as painting, collage, sculpture, or mixed media. Use these mediums to experiment and transform your emotions into creative energy. Allow yourself to explore new artistic processes and take risks in your artistic practice. Reflect on how the process of transforming emotions into creative energy affects your emotional state and artistic outcomes. Consider how artistic alchemy can serve as a catalyst for personal growth, self-expression, and emotional exploration.

Sketches and Ideas

Artistic Alchemy

Find a quiet and comfortable space where you can engage in the creative process. Take a few deep breaths to center yourself. Gather a variety of art materials and choose one to start with. Experiment with different techniques, mediums, or styles, allowing the process to guide you.

Reflect on the artistic alchemy process. Consider the emotions, surprises, and transformations that emerged as you explored different art mediums and techniques. Reflect on the unique fusion of elements and the personal meaning infused into your artwork.

Intuitive Drawing

Allowing the subconscious to guide the art-making process, expressing emotions freely and spontaneously

Set up a quiet and undisturbed space for drawing. Let go of expectations and allow your intuition to guide your hand as you create spontaneous drawings. Use various drawing materials, such as pencils, pens, or charcoal, to express your emotions freely. Reflect on the emotions, imagery, and symbolism that emerge during the intuitive drawing process. Consider how intuitive drawing allows for a direct connection with your subconscious and facilitates the expression of deep emotions and inner experiences.

Sketches and Ideas

Intuitive Drawing

Find a quiet and comfortable space to sit. Close your eyes and take a few deep breaths to center yourself. Pick up a pen, pencil, or any drawing tool. Allow your hand to move freely on the paper without judgment or preconceived ideas. Let your intuition guide your strokes and forms.

Reflect on the intuitive drawing experience. Consider the emotions, images, or symbols that emerged through your spontaneous drawing. Reflect on the messages or insights that your intuition conveyed through the artwork.

Stitching Emotions

Incorporating embroidery or sewing techniques to visually represent emotions and personal narratives

Set up a dedicated space for stitching and gather embroidery or sewing supplies. Use these materials to create stitched artworks that visually represent your emotions or personal narratives. Experiment with different stitches, patterns, and textures to convey the depth of your feelings and the essence of your stories. Reflect on the emotions and stories embedded in your stitched artworks and how the process of stitching provides a tactile and meditative experience of expressing and processing emotions.

Sketches and Ideas

Stitching Emotions

Find a quiet and comfortable space where you can engage in stitching or embroidery. Take a few deep breaths to center yourself. Choose fabric, thread, and needles. Allow your emotions to guide your needle as you stitch patterns or free-form shapes.

Reflect on the process of stitching emotions. Consider the emotions and memories that arose as you engaged in the stitching process. Reflect on the symbolism of the thread, fabric, and stitches as a means of expressing and processing emotions.

Writing in Nature

Taking the journaling practice outdoors and allowing the natural environment to inspire written expressions

Find a peaceful outdoor setting, such as a park, garden, or nature trail. Settle into the environment and connect with the sights, sounds, and sensations around you. Begin journaling, allowing the natural surroundings to inspire your written expressions. Reflect on the relationship between nature and your emotions. Consider how writing in nature enhances your connection to the natural world and provides a refreshing and reflective space for self-expression and emotional exploration.

Sketches and Ideas

Writing in Nature

Find a peaceful outdoor location, such as a park or garden. Find a comfortable spot to sit and take a few deep breaths to connect with your surroundings. Use your journal or a notebook to write freely, letting the natural environment inspire your words.

Reflect on the experience of writing in nature. Consider the emotions, sensory experiences, and connections with the natural environment that influenced your writing. Reflect on how the outdoor setting enhanced your creativity and self-expression.

Memory Boxes

Creating personalized boxes or containers to store meaningful objects that evoke memories and emotions

Gather a box or container along with meaningful objects that evoke memories and emotions. Arrange these objects in the box, creating a personalized collection of significant mementos. Reflect on the memories associated with each object and the emotions they evoke. Consider how the act of curating a memory box serves as a tangible expression of your emotions and a way to preserve and honor important moments in your life.

Sketches and Ideas

Memory Boxes

Find a quiet and comfortable space to gather meaningful objects and a box or container. Take a few deep breaths to center yourself. Select objects that hold personal significance or evoke specific memories or emotions for you. Arrange them in the memory box, considering their arrangement and any accompanying words or notes.

Reflect on the memory box creation process. Consider the emotions, memories, and connections that arose as you selected and arranged the meaningful objects. Reflect on the significance of preserving and honoring these memories and the emotions they evoke.

Collage of Dreams

Using images, symbols, and words to represent dreams and explore their deeper meanings

Collect images, symbols, and words that represent your dreams, whether literal or symbolic. Use these elements to create collages that visually capture the essence and meanings of your dreams. Reflect on the symbolism and connections between the images, symbols, and words used in your dream collages. Consider how the process of creating collages of dreams deepens your understanding of your dreams and facilitates self-reflection and exploration of your subconscious mind.

Sketches and Ideas

Collage of Dreams

Find a quiet and comfortable space where you can focus. Close your eyes and take a few deep breaths to center yourself. Reflect on your dreams and any recurring symbols or themes. Open your eyes and create a collage using images, symbols, and words that represent your dream world.

Reflect on the collage of dreams. Consider the emotions, symbols, and personal insights that emerged as you assembled the elements of your dream world collage. Reflect on the significance and hidden meanings behind the chosen images and how they relate to your dream experiences.

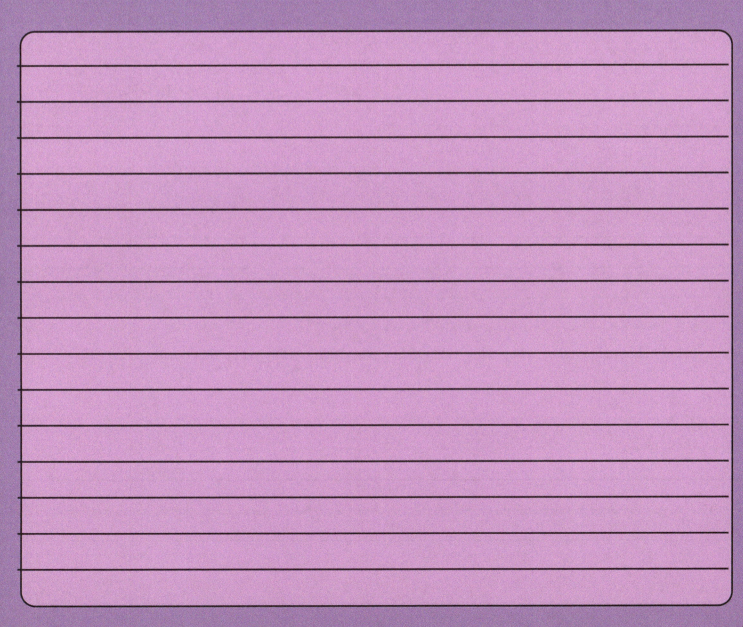

Body Movement Mapping

Using the body as a canvas to express emotions through dance, movement, or body mapping techniques

Find a spacious area where you can freely move and use your body as a canvas for self-expression. Explore different movements, gestures, or body mapping techniques to express your emotions physically. Reflect on the sensations, emotions, and messages conveyed through your body movements. Consider how body movement mapping allows for a direct and embodied expression of emotions and enhances your self-awareness and connection with your physicality.

Sketches and Ideas

Body Movement Mapping

Find a spacious area where you can move freely. Take a few deep breaths to center yourself. Start by improvising movements that reflect your emotions. Observe the way your body naturally moves and the areas it gravitates toward. Use markers or colored tape to create a map of your body's movement patterns.

Reflect on the body movement mapping process. Consider the emotions and sensations that emerged as you observed and mapped your body's movements. Reflect on any patterns, connections, or revelations that surfaced through this embodied exploration.

Art of Letting Go

Using art as a tool for releasing and processing emotions tied to loss, grief, or past experiences

Set aside dedicated time and space for art-making. Choose art materials and techniques that resonate with your emotions. Allow yourself to express and release emotions tied to loss, grief, or past experiences through your artistic process. Reflect on the emotions that arise during the art-making process and consider how the act of creating art helps in the process of letting go and finding healing or closure.

Sketches and Ideas

Art of Letting Go

Find a quiet and comfortable space where you can focus. Take a few deep breaths to center yourself. Choose an art medium that resonates with you, such as painting or drawing. As you create, let go of expectations and attachments. Allow the process to be cathartic and liberating.

Reflect on the experience of creating art as a form of letting go. Consider the emotions, thoughts, and release that came with embracing imperfection and detaching from outcomes. Reflect on the transformative power of art in the process of emotional healing and growth.

The Power of Words

Exploring the impact of affirmations, mantras, and positive self-talk through written or visual expressions

Find a quiet and focused space for reflection and introspection. Write down affirmations, mantras, or positive self-talk that resonate with your emotions and personal growth journey. Reflect on the meaning and impact of these affirmations in shaping your mindset and emotions. Consider creating visual expressions of these affirmations through calligraphy, typography, or artistic lettering to enhance their visual impact and serve as reminders of your inner strength and resilience.

Sketches and Ideas

The Power of Words

Find a quiet and comfortable space where you can reflect. Take a few deep breaths to center yourself. Select a meaningful quote or affirmation that resonates with you. Write it down or create a visual representation of the words. Reflect on the meaning and impact of the chosen words on your emotions and thoughts.

Reflect on the power of words. Consider the emotions and insights that arose as you engaged with the chosen quote or affirmation. Reflect on the ways in which words can shape our emotions, mindset, and overall well-being.

Transformative Masks

Creating masks that symbolize different emotions or aspects of the self, allowing for exploration and transformation

Gather materials such as paper, fabric, or clay to create masks. Use these materials to design and craft masks that symbolize different emotions or aspects of your self. Reflect on the emotions and facets of your identity represented by each mask. Explore how wearing and embodying these transformative masks can facilitate self-exploration, personal transformation, and the expression of different emotional states. Consider the symbolism and transformative power of masks in the context of your artistic and personal journey.

Sketches and Ideas

Transformative Masks

Find a quiet and comfortable space where you can create. Take a few deep breaths to center yourself. Gather art supplies and materials to create a mask. Reflect on the emotions, personas, or aspects of yourself that you would like to explore. Design and create a mask that represents these emotions or personas.

Reflect on the transformative masks creation process. Consider the emotions, discoveries, or insights that emerged as you crafted and wore the mask. Reflect on how the mask allowed you to embody and explore different aspects of yourself and your emotions.

Zen Doodling

Engaging in meditative doodling or repetitive mark-making as a way to calm the mind and express emotions

Find a quiet and comfortable space where you can engage in meditative doodling. Use pens, markers, or other drawing tools to create repetitive patterns, shapes, or lines. Allow the process of doodling to calm your mind and let your emotions flow through the mark-making. Reflect on the calming effect of doodling and how repetitive mark-making helps you connect with your emotions and attain a state of mindfulness and relaxation.

Sketches and Ideas

Zen Doodling

Find a quiet and comfortable space where you can focus. Take a few deep breaths to center yourself. Pick up a pen or pencil and a piece of paper. Start making repetitive and meditative marks, lines, or patterns. Allow yourself to enter a state of flow and calmness.

Reflect on the zen doodling experience. Consider the emotions, calmness, and meditative state you achieved through the repetitive marks. Reflect on the insights or feelings of tranquility that emerged as you engaged in this mindful and creative practice.

Soul Collage

Creating collages that represent different aspects of the self, allowing for self-discovery and emotional exploration

Gather a variety of images, photographs, and materials that resonate with different aspects of your identity. Use these materials to create collages that represent different facets of yourself and your emotions. Reflect on the symbolism and meanings embedded in your soul collages. Explore how the process of creating collages allows for self-discovery, introspection, and emotional exploration. Consider the connections between the visual representations in your collages and your inner world.

Sketches and Ideas

Soul Collage

Find a quiet and comfortable space to reflect. Close your eyes and take a few deep breaths to center yourself. Reflect on different aspects of yourself and the emotions they represent. Open your eyes and create collages that embody these aspects, using various images, colors, and textures.

Reflect on the soul collage process. Consider the emotions, insights, and connections that arose as you assembled the collages representing different aspects of yourself. Reflect on the integration and self-discovery fostered through this creative exploration.

Art as Self-Care

Exploring art techniques and practices that promote self-care, relaxation, and emotional well-being

Set aside dedicated time for engaging in art as a self-care practice. Explore various art techniques and practices that promote relaxation and emotional well-being, such as mindful coloring, art journaling, or intuitive painting. Reflect on how the art-making process nurtures your emotional well-being, promotes self-care, and helps you find moments of calm and inner balance. Consider how integrating art into your self-care routine enhances your overall emotional and mental well-being.

Sketches and Ideas

Art as Self-Care

Find a peaceful and comfortable space where you can focus on self-care. Take a few deep breaths to center yourself. Choose an art activity that brings you joy and relaxation, such as coloring, painting, or creating with clay. Engage in the activity mindfully, nurturing your well-being and emotions.

Reflect on the experience of using art as self-care. Consider the emotions, relaxation, and rejuvenation that came with engaging in the chosen art activity. Reflect on the significance of prioritizing self-care and the role of art in nurturing emotional well-being.

Embracing Colors

Use different hues to evoke specific emotions, express moods, and convey personal experiences through various artistic mediums

Select a range of colors that correspond to specific emotions or moods. Choose an artistic medium, such as painting, drawing, or mixed media, to explore and experiment with these colors. Create artworks that express and evoke emotions, moods, or personal experiences using the chosen color palette. Reflect on the emotions and personal meanings associated with the colors used in your artworks. Consider how color can evoke powerful emotional responses and convey personal narratives in visual art.

Sketches and Ideas

Embracing Colors

Find a quiet and comfortable space to sit. Close your eyes and take a few deep breaths to center yourself. Visualize different colors and their associated emotions. Allow these colors to wash over you and evoke specific feelings and moods.

Reflect on the emotions and sensations evoked by the different colors you visualized. Consider the ways in which colors can convey and amplify emotions, express moods, and influence your artistic expression. Reflect on any personal experiences or memories associated with specific colors.

Collage of Memories

Let the artwork serve as a visual representation of significant moments and experiences

Collect photographs, ephemera, or personal items that hold significance to your memories and experiences. Use these materials to create collages that visually represent those significant moments. Reflect on the memories and emotions evoked by the collages. Consider how the act of creating a collage of memories allows you to capture and preserve important moments in your life and provides a visual representation of your personal journey.

Sketches and Ideas

Collage of Memories

Find a peaceful and comfortable space to sit and reflect. Close your eyes and take a few deep breaths to center yourself. Reflect on significant moments and experiences that hold emotional weight for you. Open your eyes and create a collage that visually represents these memories.

Reflect on the emotions and memories that surfaced as you assembled the collage of memories. Consider the symbolism and visual elements you incorporated and how they encapsulate the essence of the significant moments and experiences. Reflect on the significance and impact of these memories in shaping your identity.

Writing Through Emotions

Use prompts and exercises to express and explore your inner world through the written word, allowing for self-reflection and emotional release

Set aside dedicated time for writing. Use prompts or exercises that encourage you to delve into your emotions and inner world through the written word. Allow yourself to freely express and explore your feelings, thoughts, and experiences through writing. Reflect on the written reflections and how they provide insights into your emotions, facilitate self-reflection, and serve as a means of emotional release and self-discovery.

Sketches and Ideas

Writing Through Emotions

Find a quiet and comfortable space where you can reflect and write. Take a few deep breaths to center yourself. Choose a writing prompt that resonates with your current emotions or experiences. Allow yourself to write freely, exploring your inner world and expressing your emotions on the page.

Reflect on the writing process and the emotions that emerged through your expressive writing. Consider the insights, self-reflection, or emotional release that writing provided. Reflect on the power of written expression as a tool for exploring and understanding your emotions.

Found Object Art

Repurpose and arrange these objects in unique ways to convey emotions, tell stories, and evoke thought-provoking responses

Collect various found objects that resonate with your emotions or have personal significance. Repurpose and arrange these objects in unique ways to create artwork that conveys emotions, tells stories, or prompts thought-provoking responses. Reflect on the emotions and narratives conveyed through the found object artworks and how they inspire introspection and evoke emotional connections in viewers. Consider the transformative power of ordinary objects when used in the context of artistic expression.

Sketches and Ideas

Found Object Art

Find a quiet and comfortable space to explore and reflect. Take a few deep breaths to center yourself. Gather a collection of objects that speak to you, such as found materials, natural elements, or personal items. Arrange and repurpose these objects in a unique way that conveys emotions, tells stories, or provokes thought.

Reflect on the found object art creation process. Consider the emotions, narratives, or thought-provoking responses that emerged as you arranged and repurposed the objects. Reflect on the symbolism and personal meaning infused into your artwork.

Nature's Inspiration

Use nature as a muse for artistic expression, whether through painting, drawing, or other mediums, allowing its inherent tranquility and vitality to ignite your creative process

Immerse yourself in nature by spending time outdoors, observing the natural surroundings, and connecting with its tranquility and vitality. Use your preferred artistic medium, such as painting, drawing, or photography, to create artworks inspired by nature. Reflect on how nature's beauty, serenity, and vitality fuel your creative process and evoke emotions and a sense of connection with the natural world. Consider how the integration of nature into art enhances your artistic expression and emotional well-being.

Sketches and Ideas

Nature's Inspiration

Find a tranquil outdoor setting that inspires you. Take a moment to connect with your breath and the natural surroundings. Engage with nature through activities such as painting, drawing, or photography, allowing its tranquility and vitality to fuel your creative process.

Reflect on the experience of creating art in nature. Consider the emotions, inspiration, and connection with the natural environment that influenced your artistic expression. Reflect on how nature's beauty and energy enhanced your creativity and emotional well-being.

Dancing Emotions

Use dance as a means to channel and release emotions, expressing yourself through graceful or energetic movements that embody the depth of your feelings .

Create a safe and spacious area for dancing. Choose music that resonates with your emotions. Allow yourself to move freely and intuitively, expressing your emotions through graceful or energetic dance movements. Reflect on the sensations, emotions, and release experienced during the dance session. Consider how dance allows for a nonverbal expression of emotions and how it promotes physical and emotional well-being.

Sketches and Ideas

Dancing Emotions

Find a spacious and unobstructed area where you can move freely. Take a few deep breaths to center yourself. Play music that resonates with your emotions. Allow your body to express and release emotions through graceful or energetic movements.

Reflect on the emotions, sensations, and release experienced during your dancing session. Consider the ways in which movement and dance allow for emotional expression and how they serve as a powerful means of embodying and communicating your feelings.

Poetry Corner

Write heartfelt poems, experiment with different styles and forms, and explore the beauty of language as a means of self-expression

Set aside dedicated time for writing poetry. Explore different styles and forms of poetry, experiment with poetic techniques, and let your creativity flow in expressing your emotions through heartfelt poems. Reflect on the beauty and power of language as a means of self-expression and emotional exploration. Consider how poetry allows for the fusion of emotions and words, inviting readers or listeners to connect with the depth of your feelings and experiences.

Sketches and Ideas

Poetry Corner

Find a quiet and comfortable space to reflect and write. Take a few deep breaths to center yourself. Reflect on your emotions and experiences, and use different styles and forms of poetry to explore the beauty of language as a means of self-expression.

Reflect on the poems you wrote in the poetry corner. Consider the emotions, imagery, and language that you used to convey your feelings. Reflect on the power of poetry to capture and communicate emotions, as well as the insights and connections made through this creative exploration.

Musical Musings

Reflect on the emotions stirred by various melodies, lyrics, or genres, and use them as a catalyst for personal artistic exploration and introspection

Listen to different genres of music or specific songs that evoke emotions within you. Reflect on the emotions, memories, or thoughts stirred by the melodies, lyrics, or overall musical experience. Use these musical musings as a catalyst for personal artistic exploration and introspection. Consider how music can serve as a powerful emotional trigger and source of inspiration for creative expression.

Sketches and Ideas

Musical Musings

Find a quiet and comfortable space where you can focus. Take a few deep breaths to center yourself. Choose music that resonates with your emotions and listen attentively. Reflect on the emotions stirred by the melodies, lyrics, or genres, and use them as a catalyst for personal artistic exploration and introspection.

Reflect on the emotions and thoughts evoked by the music you listened to. Consider how the music influenced your state of mind, creativity, and self-reflection. Reflect on any personal connections or memories associated with the chosen music and how they intersected with your emotions.

Expressive Writing

Use descriptive language, storytelling techniques, and personal narratives to convey emotions and delve into self-discovery

Set aside dedicated time for expressive writing. Use descriptive language, storytelling techniques, and personal narratives to convey your emotions and delve into self-discovery through the written word. Reflect on the written expressions, the insights gained, and the emotions conveyed through expressive writing. Consider how expressive writing can be a therapeutic tool for emotional exploration, self-reflection, and personal growth.

Sketches and Ideas

Expressive Writing

Find a peaceful and comfortable space where you can focus on writing. Take a few deep breaths to center yourself. Use descriptive language, storytelling techniques, and personal narratives to convey emotions and delve into self-discovery.

Reflect on the writing process and the emotions, stories, or personal insights that emerged through your expressive writing. Consider the power of descriptive language in capturing and expressing emotions, as well as the ways in which writing promotes self-discovery and emotional exploration.

Sculpting Emotions

Explore the three-dimensional realm, creating tactile artwork that captures the essence of your feelings and allows for a tangible expression of emotions

Set up a sculpting workspace with clay or other sculpting materials. Use these materials to create three-dimensional artworks that capture the essence of your feelings. Allow your hands to mold and shape the sculptures, expressing emotions through tactile art. Reflect on the sensations, emotions, and the tangible expression of emotions achieved through sculpting. Consider how sculpting provides a unique medium for translating emotions into physical forms and exploring the relationship between touch and emotions.

Sketches and Ideas

Sculpting Emotions

Find a quiet and comfortable space where you can engage in sculpting or modeling with clay. Take a few deep breaths to center yourself. Allow the clay to guide your hands as you create three-dimensional artwork that captures the essence of your feelings.

Reflect on the process of sculpting emotions. Consider the emotions, tactile sensations, and symbolism that arose as you worked with clay to express and shape your feelings. Reflect on the transformative and tangible nature of sculpting emotions through art.

Imaginary Landscapes

Use your artistic skills to bring fantastical worlds to life, visually expressing the depth and nuances of your innermost landscapes

Engage your imagination and artistic skills to create imaginary landscapes on paper or canvas. Use colors, textures, and composition to visually express the depth and nuances of your innermost landscapes. Reflect on the imagery and emotions evoked by the imaginary landscapes you create. Consider how the process of bringing fantastical worlds to life through art allows for an exploration of your inner world and the representation of emotions and dreams.

Sketches and Ideas

Imaginary Landscapes

Find a quiet and comfortable space where you can focus on visualization. Take a few deep breaths to center yourself. Use your artistic skills to create vivid and fantastical worlds that visually express the depth and nuances of your innermost landscapes.

Reflect on the imaginary landscapes you created. Consider the emotions, imagery, and symbolism that emerged as you brought these fantastical worlds to life. Reflect on the insights and personal meaning encapsulated within the landscapes you envisioned and visualized.

Photography Journey

Capture moments, scenes, and details that resonate with your emotions, using the camera as a tool to document and explore the world around you and within you

Take your camera or smartphone and embark on a photography journey. Capture moments, scenes, or details that resonate with your emotions. Use photography as a tool to document and explore the world around you and within you. Reflect on the photographs you capture and the emotions they evoke. Consider how photography allows you to see and interpret the world through an emotional lens and how it facilitates self-expression and visual storytelling.

Sketches and Ideas

Photography Journey

Find a quiet and peaceful space where you can observe and reflect. Take a few deep breaths to center yourself. Use the camera as a tool to capture moments, scenes, and details that resonate with your emotions, allowing you to document and explore the world around you and within you.

Reflect on the photographs you took during your photography journey. Consider the emotions, stories, or reflections captured in each image. Reflect on the ways in which photography serves as a medium for expressing emotions and uncovering hidden aspects of yourself and the world.

Expressive Letter Writing

Use the power of words in letter writing as a therapeutic tool for emotional expression

Set aside dedicated time for letter writing. Write heartfelt letters to yourself, loved ones, or even fictional characters, expressing your emotions and thoughts. Use the power of words to convey your deepest emotions and experiences. Reflect on the emotional release and self-discovery achieved through expressive letter writing. Consider how writing letters allows you to express yourself honestly and intimately, nurturing emotional connection and self-expression.

Sketches and Ideas

Expressive Letter Writing

Find a quiet and comfortable space to reflect and write. Take a few deep breaths to center yourself. Use the power of words in letter writing as a therapeutic tool for emotional expression. Choose a recipient, whether real or imagined, and let your emotions flow onto the page.

Reflect on the experience of writing expressive letters. Consider the emotions, thoughts, and catharsis that came with pouring your emotions onto the page. Reflect on the healing potential of letter writing and the ways in which it allows for emotional release and connection.

Personal Symbols

Use these symbols in your artistic expressions to convey deeper meaning and connection with your inner world

Explore and identify personal symbols that hold meaning to you. Use these symbols in your artistic expressions to convey deeper emotions, thoughts, or connections with your inner world. Reflect on the personal significance and the emotions evoked by these symbols. Consider how the integration of personal symbols enhances the depth and personal resonance of your artistic expressions.

Sketches and Ideas

Personal Symbols

Find a quiet and comfortable space to reflect. Close your eyes and take a few deep breaths to center yourself. Reflect on personal symbols that hold meaning and connection to your inner world. Use these symbols in your artistic expressions to convey deeper meaning and evoke emotions.

Reflect on the personal symbols you incorporated into your artistic expressions. Consider the emotions, memories, and connections that these symbols evoke within you. Reflect on the significance of personal symbols as a means of self-expression and their ability to communicate emotions and experiences.

Abstract Expression

Use colors, shapes, and textures to communicate your feelings and allow viewers to interpret and connect with your art on a personal level

Embrace abstraction in your art practice. Use colors, shapes, and textures to communicate your feelings and emotions. Allow viewers to interpret and connect with your art on a personal level. Reflect on the emotions expressed through abstract art and the ways in which viewers engage with and interpret your artwork. Consider how abstract expression enables a unique and personal form of communication that transcends explicit representation and fosters emotional connection.

Sketches and Ideas

Abstract Expression

Find a quiet and comfortable space where you can focus on creating art. Take a few deep breaths to center yourself. Use colors, shapes, and textures to communicate your feelings through abstract art. Allow viewers to interpret and connect with your art on a personal level.

Reflect on the abstract expression process. Consider the emotions, interpretations, or connections that your abstract art evokes in viewers. Reflect on the power of abstract art to communicate emotions beyond literal representation and the ways in which it invites personal interpretation and engagement.

Inspirational Quotes

Seek inspiration from meaningful quotes that resonate with your emotions

Collect and compile a collection of meaningful quotes that resonate with your emotions. Reflect on these quotes and explore how they evoke different emotions within you. Use these quotes as a source of inspiration for your artistic creations. Consider how the combination of quotes and art enhances the emotional resonance and deeper meanings conveyed in your artwork.

Sketches and Ideas

Inspirational Quotes

Find a quiet and comfortable space to reflect and write. Take a few deep breaths to center yourself. Seek inspiration from meaningful quotes that resonate with your emotions. Reflect on the quote that resonates with you the most and explore the emotions and insights it evokes within you.

Reflect on the inspirational quote that resonated with you. Consider the emotions, thoughts, or realizations that emerged as you reflected on the quote's meaning and its impact on your emotions and mindset. Reflect on how the quote inspires your artistic exploration and personal growth.

Puppetry Therapy

Use puppets as a means to express emotions, convey narratives, and delve into the complexities of human experiences in a safe and imaginative way

Create or gather puppets and engage in puppetry therapy. Use the puppets as a means to express emotions, convey narratives, and explore the complexities of human experiences in a safe and imaginative way. Reflect on the emotions and narratives that emerge during the puppetry therapy sessions. Consider how puppetry allows for a playful and imaginative exploration of emotions and human experiences.

Sketches and Ideas

Puppetry Therapy

Find a quiet and comfortable space where you can engage in puppetry. Take a few deep breaths to center yourself. Use puppets as a means to express emotions, convey narratives, and delve into the complexities of human experiences in a safe and imaginative way.

Reflect on the puppetry therapy experience. Consider the emotions, narratives, or insights that emerged as you engaged with the puppets. Reflect on the role of imagination and play in processing emotions and gaining a deeper understanding of the human experience.

Dream Journaling

Dive into the realm of dreams and their emotional significance

Set up a dedicated space for dream journaling. Record and explore your dreams in a journal. Reflect on the emotional significance and symbolism within your dreams. Consider how dream journaling allows you to delve into the realm of dreams, connect with your subconscious, and explore the emotions and meanings embedded in your dreams.

Sketches and Ideas

Dream Journaling

Find a quiet and comfortable space where you can reflect and write. Take a few deep breaths to center yourself. Dive into the realm of dreams and their emotional significance. Use your journal to explore and document your dreams, reflecting on the emotions and symbolism they hold.

Reflect on the dreams you journaled about. Consider the emotions, symbolism, or insights that surfaced through your dream exploration. Reflect on the ways in which dreams can provide a window into your subconscious and the valuable information they offer for emotional growth and self-understanding.

Artistic Self-Portraits

Use various artistic techniques to portray yourself, exploring the complexities and uniqueness of your identity

Engage in self-portrait art-making. Use various artistic techniques, such as drawing, painting, or mixed media, to portray yourself and explore the complexities and uniqueness of your identity. Reflect on the emotions, thoughts, or aspects of your identity expressed in your self-portraits. Consider how self-portraiture can serve as a means of self-exploration, self-expression, and self-empowerment.

Sketches and Ideas

Artistic Self-Portraits

Find a quiet and comfortable space where you can reflect and create art. Take a few deep breaths to center yourself. Use various artistic techniques to portray yourself, exploring the complexities and uniqueness of your identity. Allow the process to be a form of self-discovery.

Reflect on the artistic self-portraits you created. Consider the emotions, self-perception, or aspects of your identity that emerged as you explored different artistic techniques. Reflect on the transformative and introspective nature of creating self-portraits.

Healing Mandalas

Use sacred geometric patterns, intricate designs, and meaningful symbols to facilitate relaxation, self-reflection, and the channeling of positive energy

Create mandalas with sacred geometric patterns, intricate designs, and meaningful symbols. Use the creation of mandalas as a practice to facilitate relaxation, self-reflection, and the channeling of positive energy. Reflect on the calming and centering effects of creating mandalas. Consider how the symbolism and patterns in mandalas help in the exploration of emotions and the cultivation of positive energy.

Sketches and Ideas

Healing Mandalas

Find a quiet and comfortable space where you can focus on creating mandalas. Take a few deep breaths to center yourself. Use sacred geometric patterns, intricate designs, and meaningful symbols to facilitate relaxation, self-reflection, and the channeling of positive energy.

Reflect on the healing mandalas you created. Consider the emotions, relaxation, or self-reflection that emerged as you engaged with the meditative process of creating mandalas. Reflect on the transformative power of mandalas in promoting emotional well-being and balance.

Personal Growth Collage

Reflect on your personal growth journey through collage art

Collect images, words, and materials that symbolize your personal growth journey. Use these materials to create collages that visually represent your journey. Reflect on the milestones, challenges, and emotions associated with your personal growth. Consider how the process of creating personal growth collages allows you to acknowledge and celebrate your progress while also contemplating the lessons learned along the way.

Sketches and Ideas

Personal Growth Collage

Find a quiet and comfortable space where you can reflect and create a collage. Take a few deep breaths to center yourself. Reflect on your personal growth journey and select images, words, and symbols that represent your progress and milestones. Arrange them in a collage that reflects your growth and transformation.

Reflect on the personal growth collage you created. Consider the emotions, memories, or realizations that arose as you selected and arranged the elements. Reflect on the transformative nature of your personal growth journey and the symbolism embedded within the collage.

Gratitude Art

Express gratitude through artistic creations

Set aside dedicated time for creating art focused on gratitude. Use art materials and techniques to create artworks that express gratitude. Reflect on the things, experiences, or people you are grateful for and how the act of creating gratitude art enhances your appreciation and emotional well-being. Consider how gratitude art can serve as a reminder of the positive aspects of life and a means of cultivating a grateful mindset.

Sketches and Ideas

Gratitude Art

Find a peaceful and comfortable space where you can focus on gratitude. Take a few deep breaths to center yourself. Use artistic creations as a medium for expressing gratitude. Reflect on the blessings, experiences, or people you are grateful for, and create art that embodies your gratitude.

Reflect on the gratitude art you created. Consider the emotions, thoughts, or connections with gratitude that arose as you expressed your appreciation through art. Reflect on the transformative power of gratitude and its ability to foster emotional well-being and perspective.

Additional Notes and Reflections

Additional Notes and Reflections

Additional Notes and Reflections

Additional Notes and Reflections

Additional Notes and Reflections

Additional Notes and Reflections

Additional Notes and Reflections

Additional Notes and Reflections

Additional Notes and Reflections

Additional Notes and Reflections

Printed in the USA
CPSIA information can be obtained
at www.ICGtesting.com
LVHW082005180724
785773LV00006B/864